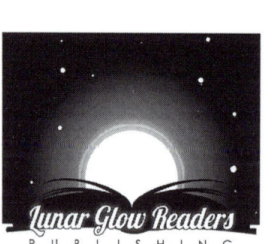

All rights reserved. No part of this book may be reproduced or transmitted in any form by any means, electronic or mechanical, including photocopying, scanning and recording, or by any information storage and retrieval system, without permission in writing from the publisher, except for the review for inclusion in a magazine , newpaper or broadcast.

Cover and page design by Lunar Glow Studios - Copyright 2017

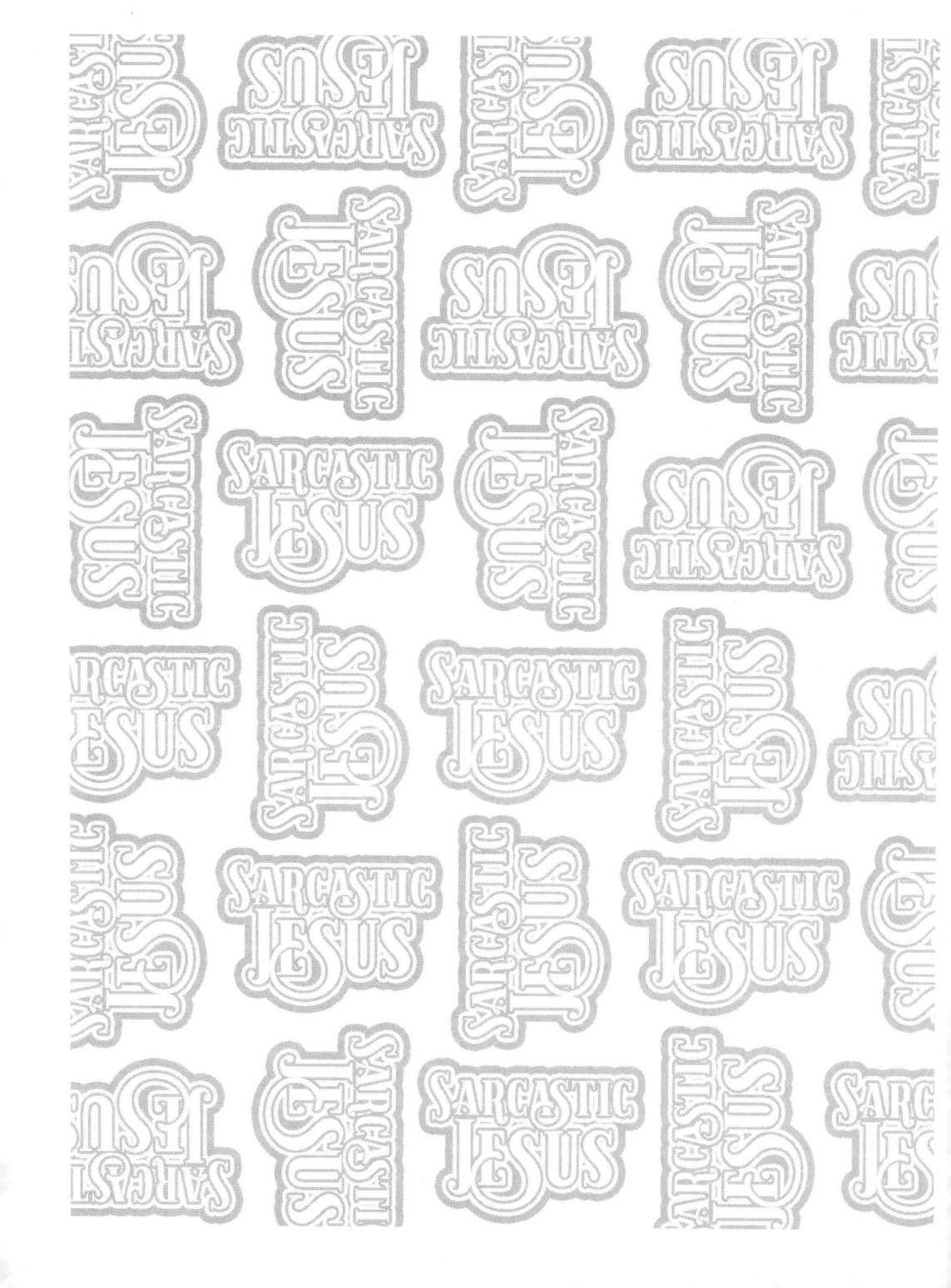

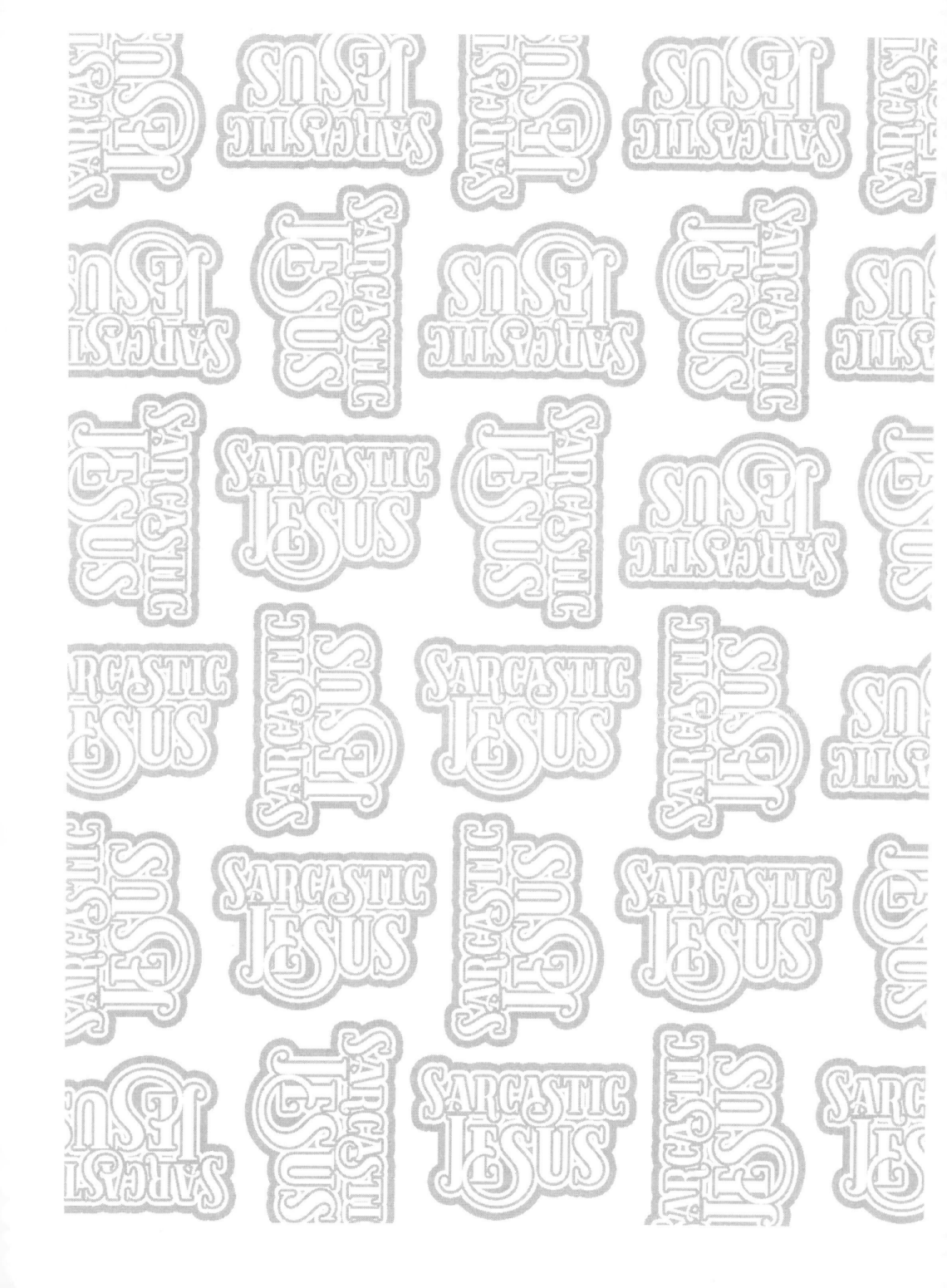

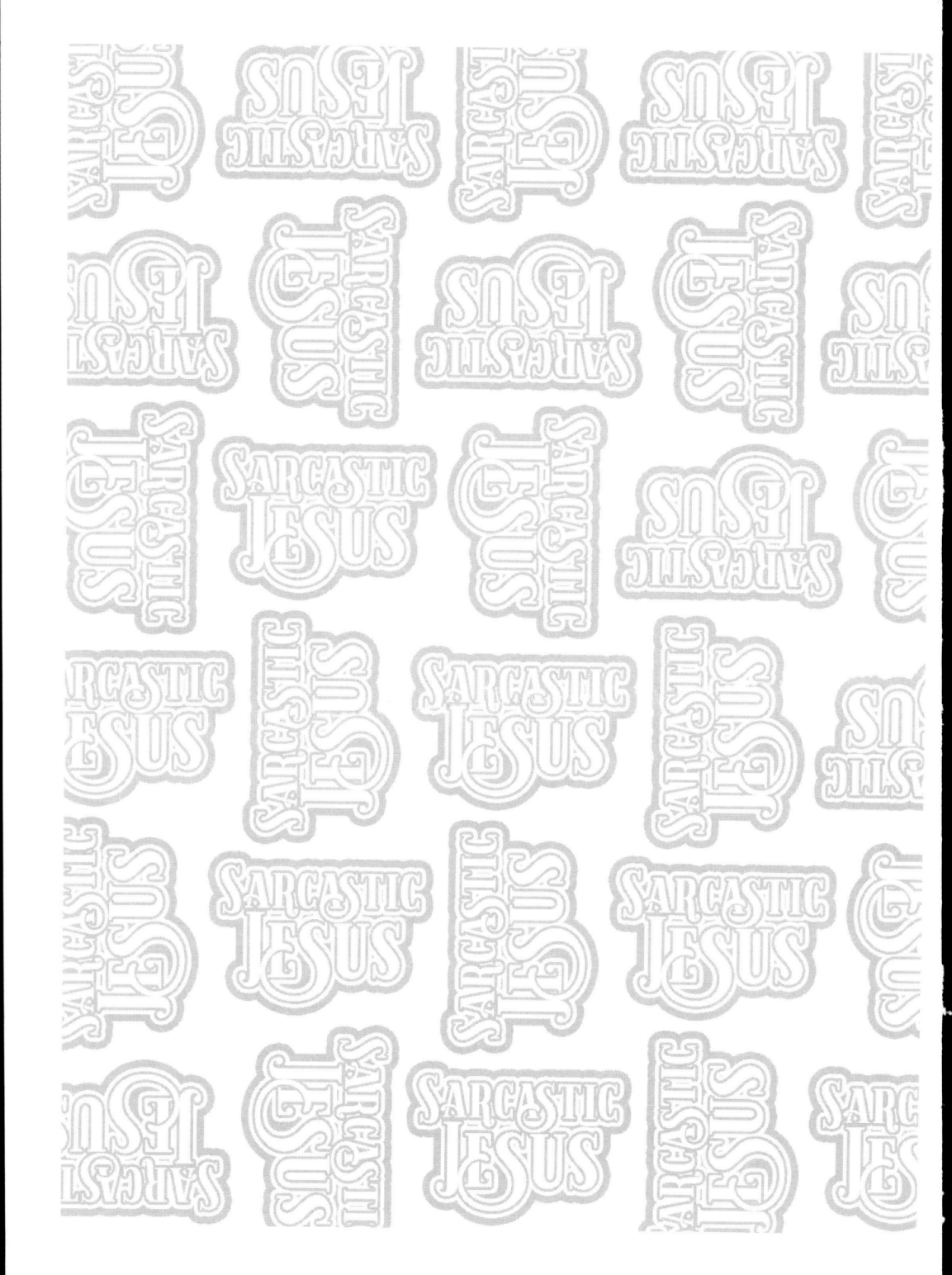

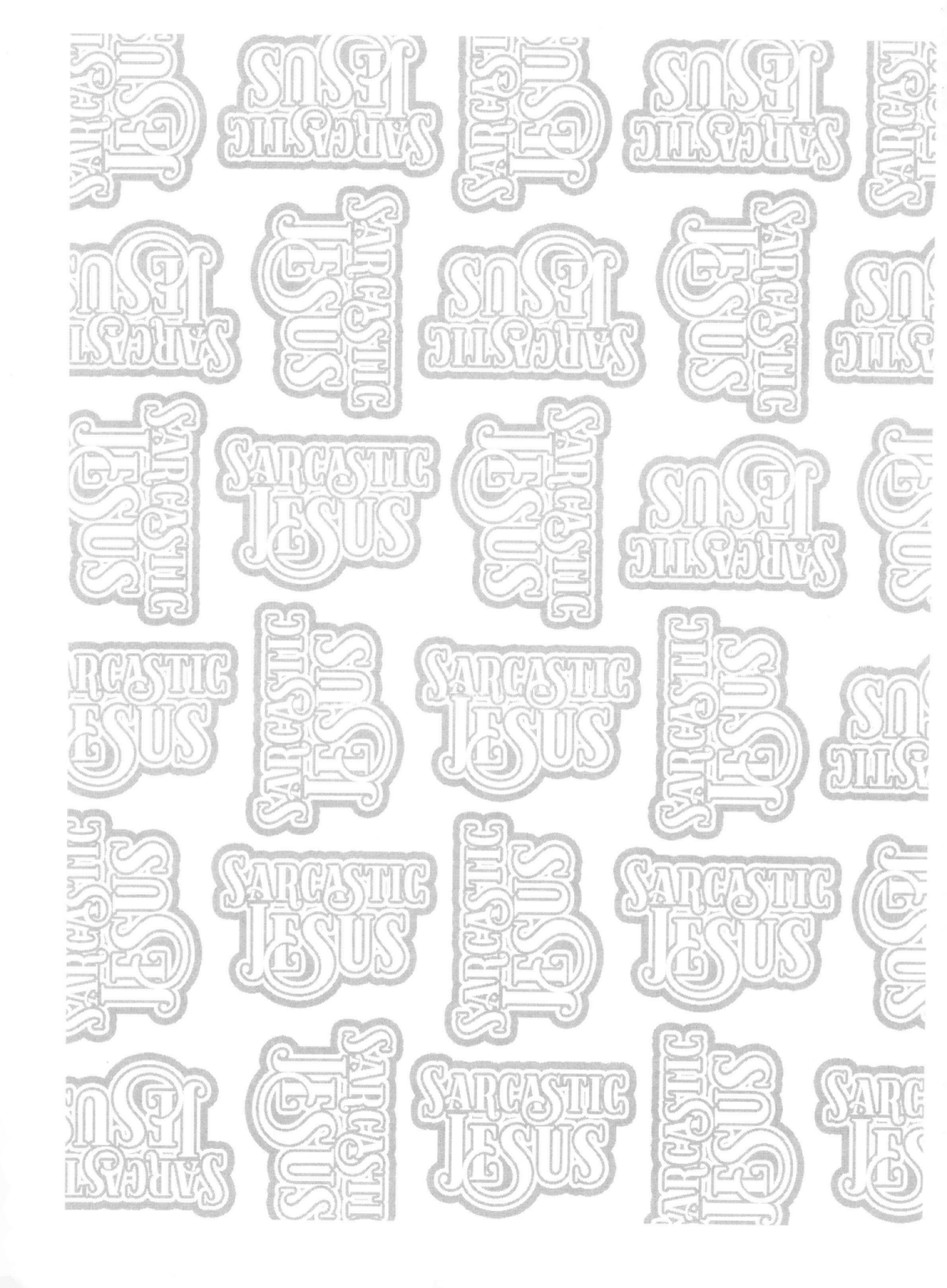

Made in the USA
Middletown, DE
02 December 2020